WHSmith

Practise

Number and Calculations

KS2 MATHS

Age 9–11

Richard Cooper

Advice for parents

The *Practise* Maths books are designed to practise and consolidate children's work in school. They are intended for children to complete on their own, but you may like to work with them for the first few pages.

- Don't let your child do too much at once. 'Little and often' is a good way to start.
- Reward your child with lots of praise and encouragement. These should be enjoyable activities for them.
- Discuss with your child what they have learned and what they can do.
- The **'Get ready'** section provides a gentle warm-up for the topic covered in the unit.
- The **'Let's practise'** section is usually the main activity. This section helps to consolidate understanding of the topic. The questions in this section get progressively harder.
- The **'Have a go'** section is often a challenge or something interesting that your child can go away and do which is related to the topic. It may require your child to use everyday objects around the home.
- The **'How have I done?'** section at the end of the book is a short informal test that should be attempted when all the units have been completed. It is useful for spotting any gaps in knowledge, which can then be revisited at a suitable moment.

Number and Calculations are obviously a key part of mathematics.

By the end of Year 6 most children should be able to:

- Use decimal notation for tenths, hundredths and thousandths; partition, round and order decimals with up to three places.
- Express a larger whole number as a fraction of a smaller one.
- Simplify fractions and order fractions.
- Express one quantity as a percentage of another; find equivalent fractions, decimals and percentages.
- Solve simple problems involving proportion by scaling quantities up and down.
- Use multiplication and division facts involving decimals (e.g. 0.7×5, $3.6 \div 2$).
- Use approximations and inverse operations to estimate and check results.
- Calculate mentally with whole numbers and decimals.
- Relate fractions to multiplication and division (e.g. $\frac{8}{2} = \frac{1}{2}$ of $8 = 8 \times \frac{1}{2}$).
- Find fractions and percentages of whole number quantities (e.g. 65% of £260).
- Use a calculator to solve problems involving multi-step calculations.

First published 2007
exclusively for WHSmith by
Hodder Education, part of Hachette Livre UK,
338 Euston Road
London
NW1 3BH

Impression number   10 9 8 7 6 5 4 3 2
Year   2008
Text and illustrations © Hodder Education 2007

A CIP record for this book is available from the British Library.

Cover illustration: Sally Newton Illustrations
Character illustrations: Beehive Illustration
All other illustrations: Simon Dennett at SD Illustration, Arthur Pickering and Kelly Gray
Typeset by Florence Production Ltd, Stoodleigh, Devon

ISBN   978 0 340 94334 2

Printed and bound in Spain

Contents

Welcome to Kids Club!

Hi, readers. My name's Charlie and I run Kids Club with my friend Abbie. Kids Club is an after-school club which is very similar to one somewhere near you.

We'd love you to come and join our club and see what we get up to!

I'm Abbie. Let's meet the kids who will work with you on the activities in this book.

My name's Jamelia. I look forward to Kids Club every day. The sports and games are my favourites, especially on Kids Camp in the school holidays.

Hi, I'm Megan. I've made friends with all the kids at Kids Club. I like the outings and trips we go on the best.

Hello, my name's Kim. Kids Club is a great place to chill out after school. My best friend is Alfie – he's a bit naughty but he means well!

I'm Amina. I like to do my homework at Kids Club. Charlie and Abbie are always very helpful. We're like one big happy family.

Greetings, readers, my name's Alfie! Everybody knows me here. Come and join our club; we'll have a wicked time together!

Now you've met us all, tell us something about yourself.
All the kids filled in a '**Personal Profile**' when they joined. Here's one for you to complete.

Personal Profile

INSERT PHOTO OF YOURSELF HERE

Name: ______________________________

Age: ____

School: ____________________________

Home town: ___________________________

Best friend: ___________________

My favourite:

- Book __________________
- Film ___________________
- Food __________________
- Sport __________________

My hero is ________________ because ________________

____

When I grow up I want to be a _________________________

If I ruled the world the first thing I would do is _____________

____

If I could be any celebrity for a day I would be _____________

____

1: Partitioning

The Kids Club raised some money for our local hospital. We did a sponsored times table test and raised £96.52!

Each of the digits represents an amount.

9	6	.	5	2
↓	↓		↓	↓
£90	£6		50p	2p

Charlie said he would round the sum up to the nearest ten pounds, so we gave a total of £100 to the hospital.

Get ready

For each of these amounts, write the number of pounds and number of pence.

The first one has been done for you.

1 £8.65   =   8 pounds and   65 pence
2 £22.41   =   ____ pounds and ____ pence
3 £61.77   =   ____ pounds and ____ pence
4 £89.88   =   ____ pounds and ____ pence
5 £107.90 =   ____ pounds and ____ pence
6 £225.51 =   ____ pounds and ____ pence
7 £312.21 =   ____ pounds and ____ pence
8 £199.99 =   ____ pounds and ____ pence
9 £88.08   =   ____ pounds and ____ pence
10 £501.75 =   ____ pounds and ____ pence

 ## Let's practise

Show how much each digit represents and round the sum to the nearest pound.

The first one has been done for you.

⑪ £21.89 = £20 + £1 + 80p + 9p rounded to £22
⑫ £13.75 = _____ + _____ + _____ + _____ rounded to _____
⑬ £52.88 = _____ + _____ + _____ + _____ rounded to _____
⑭ £72.71 = _____ + _____ + _____ + _____ rounded to _____
⑮ £94.26 = _____ + _____ + _____ + _____ rounded to _____
⑯ £81.45 = _____ + _____ + _____ + _____ rounded to _____
⑰ £35.94 = _____ + _____ + _____ + _____ rounded to _____
⑱ £68.10 = _____ + _____ + _____ + _____ rounded to _____
⑲ £49.57 = _____ + _____ + _____ + _____ rounded to _____
⑳ £11.33 = _____ + _____ + _____ + _____ rounded to _____

 ## Have a go

This is something to try at a shop or the supermarket. It's tricky but good fun.

When an item is scanned at the till, watch the price on the screen or display.

Mentally round the price up or down to the nearest pound.

Add up the pounds in your head as the items are scanned. You have to keep up, so concentrate.

See how close you can get to the final total.

I got it exactly right once – my Mum couldn't believe it!

2: Equivalent fractions

My Dad said he will give me $\frac{1}{2}$ of £6 if I practise my singing in the garden shed or $\frac{4}{8}$ of £6 if I don't sing at all!

Which amount is more?

Your Dad is trying to confuse you. $\frac{1}{2}$ and $\frac{4}{8}$ are the same – they are 'equivalent fractions'.

Get ready

Look at this equivalent fractions chart.

Write down the four fractions on the chart that are equivalent to one half ($\frac{1}{2}$).

1 —

2 —

3 —

4 —

1 WHOLE									
$\frac{1}{2}$					$\frac{1}{2}$				
$\frac{1}{3}$			$\frac{1}{3}$			$\frac{1}{3}$			
$\frac{1}{4}$		$\frac{1}{4}$			$\frac{1}{4}$		$\frac{1}{4}$		
$\frac{1}{5}$		$\frac{1}{5}$		$\frac{1}{5}$		$\frac{1}{5}$		$\frac{1}{5}$	
$\frac{1}{6}$	$\frac{1}{6}$		$\frac{1}{6}$		$\frac{1}{6}$		$\frac{1}{6}$		$\frac{1}{6}$
$\frac{1}{7}$	$\frac{1}{7}$	$\frac{1}{7}$		$\frac{1}{7}$		$\frac{1}{7}$		$\frac{1}{7}$	$\frac{1}{7}$
$\frac{1}{8}$	$\frac{1}{8}$	$\frac{1}{8}$	$\frac{1}{8}$		$\frac{1}{8}$	$\frac{1}{8}$	$\frac{1}{8}$		$\frac{1}{8}$
$\frac{1}{9}$	$\frac{1}{9}$	$\frac{1}{9}$	$\frac{1}{9}$	$\frac{1}{9}$	$\frac{1}{9}$	$\frac{1}{9}$	$\frac{1}{9}$	$\frac{1}{9}$	
$\frac{1}{10}$	$\frac{1}{10}$	$\frac{1}{10}$	$\frac{1}{10}$	$\frac{1}{10}$	$\frac{1}{10}$	$\frac{1}{10}$	$\frac{1}{10}$	$\frac{1}{10}$	$\frac{1}{10}$

Let's practise

Study the chart and answer these questions.

5 One third is the same as _____ and _____

6 Two eighths is the same as _____

7 Two fifths is the same as _____

8 Two thirds is the same as _____ and _____

9 Six eighths is the same as _____

10 Which row of fractions has no equivalent (apart from 1 whole) on the chart?

_____

Have a go

Learn the equivalent fractions so that you recognise them instantly.

Here are a few common ones which are useful to know.

$$\frac{1}{2} = \frac{2}{4} = \frac{3}{6} = \frac{4}{8} = \frac{5}{10}$$

$$\frac{1}{3} = \frac{2}{6} = \frac{3}{9} = \frac{4}{12} = \frac{5}{15}$$

$$\frac{1}{4} = \frac{2}{8} = \frac{3}{12} = \frac{4}{16} = \frac{5}{20}$$

I put them into a song to help me learn them. My Dad loved it!

3: Percentages

I scored 85 percent for my Maths test. Is that good?

That's very good, Kim! Percent means 'out of a hundred', so you scored $\frac{85}{100}$ or 85%.

Get ready

Write these fractions as percentages.

1. $\frac{60}{100}$ _____

2. $\frac{75}{100}$ _____

3. $\frac{30}{100}$ _____

4. $\frac{25}{100}$ _____

5. $\frac{40}{100}$ _____

6. $\frac{5}{100}$ _____

7. $\frac{15}{100}$ _____

8. $\frac{95}{100}$ _____

9. $\frac{50}{100}$ _____

10. $\frac{10}{100}$ _____

Let's practise

Look at these 100-block grids.
What percentage of each one is coloured in?

11 _____

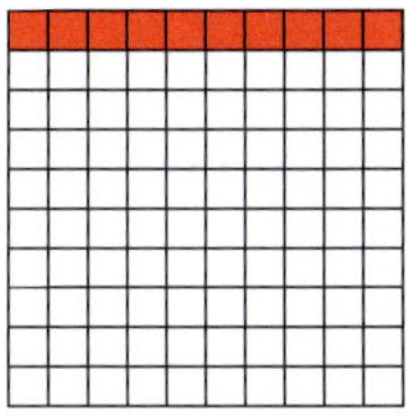

12 _____

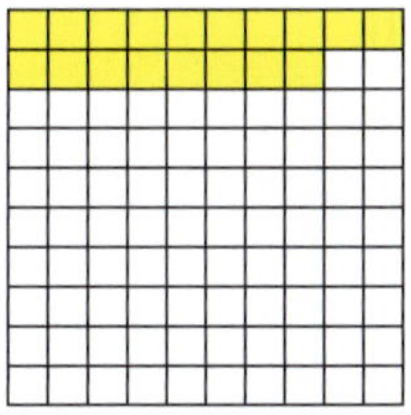

13 _____

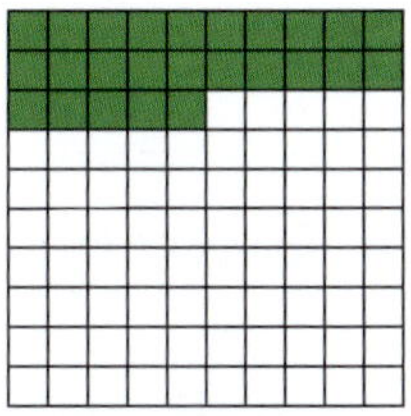

14 _____

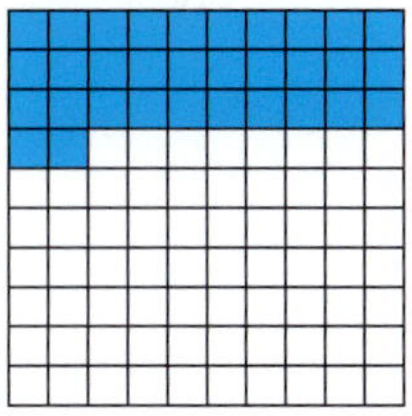

15 _____

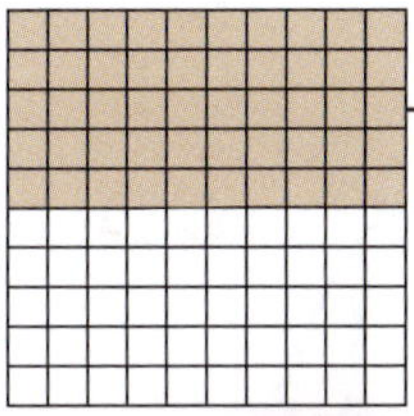

16 _____

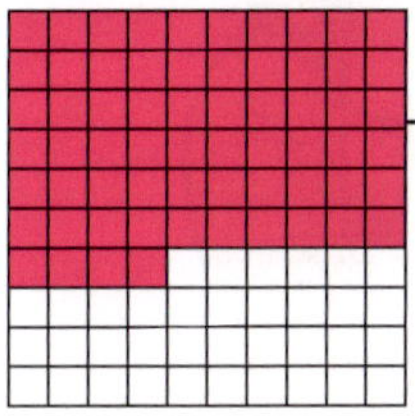

17 _____

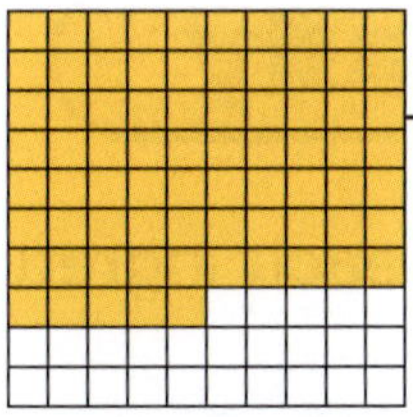

18 _____

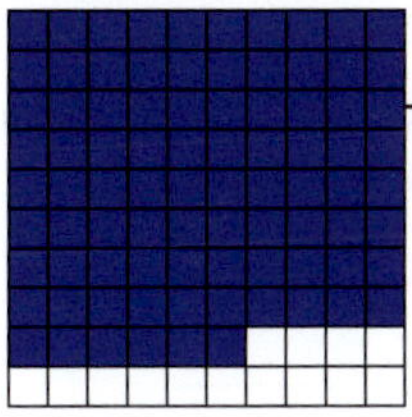

Have a go

Using books or the Internet, find a list of 'top 100 singles' or songs – or you could try films. Work out the percentage that you have seen or heard.

I've been watching the chefs on TV. This cooking lark is a piece of cake! (Or a trifle easy, in this case.)

Here are the ingredients for **Alfie's Trifle Tower (for 6 people)**

12 trifle sponges
8 cups of whipped cream
8 cups of custard
4 cans of fruit cocktail
16 glacé cherries

Get ready

1 How much of each ingredient is needed to make a Trifle Tower for **12 people**?

Trifle sponges _____
Cups of whipped cream _____
Cups of custard _____
Cans of fruit cocktail _____
Glacé cherries _____

2 Now write down the amounts of each ingredient needed to make a Trifle Tower for **3 people**.

Trifle sponges _____
Cups of whipped cream _____
Cups of custard _____
Cans of fruit cocktail _____
Glacé cherries _____

Let's practise

Now for some proper cooking. Here is a list of ingredients for my 'special of the day'.

Chicken à la Alf (serves 4)
1.6 kg of chicken
300 ml of chicken stock
4 carrots
2 onions
50 g of butter
80 g of plain flour
Cooking time = 1 hour 20 minutes

3 I would like to cook 'Chicken à la Alf' for 8 people. Can you change the amount of each ingredient so that I cook enough food?

Chicken _____

Chicken stock _____

Carrots _____

Onions _____

Butter _____

Plain flour _____

Suppose I have to increase the cooking time by the same proportion.

How long will the dish take to cook now? _____

Cut out some simple recipes from newspapers and magazines. Alter the ingredients for different numbers of people. If the recipe is for 4 people, then make it for 2, 6 or 8 people.

Imagine you had to cook for 40 people at a wedding or a party. How much of each ingredient would you need then?

5: Dealing with decimals (1)

I used to find decimals confusing (amongst lots of other things).

Charlie and Abbie helped me at Kids Club, so now it's easy. Well, I get the point anyway!

The decimal point separates whole numbers from the tenths and hundredths.

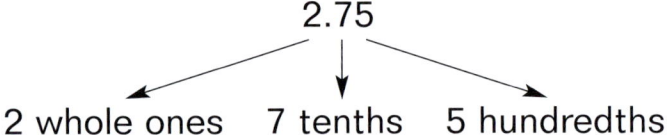

2.75

2 whole ones   7 tenths   5 hundredths

To make it easier to double and halve decimals, we can pretend the decimal point isn't there. Remember, it doesn't actually move anywhere.

Double 1.6 looks like double 16 which is 32. So, double 1.6 is 3.2

Half of 2.4 looks like half of 24 which is 12. So, half of 2.4 is 1.2

Get ready

Double these decimals.

① 3.4 _____

② 4.2 _____

③ 1.8 _____

④ 2.5 _____

⑤ 5.0 _____

Halve these decimals.

⑥ 2.2 _____

⑦ 4.8 _____

⑧ 3.6 _____

⑨ 5.4 _____

⑩ 6.2 _____

Let's practise

The money we use is counted in the decimal system.

Now try these – they're a bit harder.

Double these money decimals.

11 £1.25 _____

12 £2.30 _____

13 £3.43 _____

14 £5.18 _____

15 £4.24 _____

Halve these money decimals.

16 £6.44 _____

17 £8.60 _____

18 £10.26 _____

19 £4.82 _____

20 What is £16.70

a) doubled _____

b) halved? _____

Have a go

Imagine you have £1.50 pocket money. Alfie says that if he spins a coin and it is heads you must give him half of your pocket money. If it is tails he will double your pocket money.

Do you think this is a good deal? Explain your answer.

6: Factors and multiples

Factors? Do you think I have the 'X-factor'?

I have misunderstood! Charlie says in Maths, a **factor** is a number which exactly divides into another number.

For example, 3 is a factor of 6 because 6 can be divided exactly by 3. The other factors of 6 are 1, 2 and 6.

A **multiple** is a number that may be divided by another number without a remainder.

For example, 10 and 15 are both multiples of 5.

Get ready

All whole numbers can be divided by 1 and themselves.

Write down all the factors of these numbers.

1   4 _____

2   8 _____

3   16 _____

4   20 _____

5   32 _____

Write down all the factors of these bigger numbers.

6   64 _____

7   38 _____

8   42 _____

9   56 _____

10   100 _____

Let's practise

Here are some tips to find out whether a number is a multiple of another number. Some of them are very clever.

- Multiples of 2: the last digit is even. (32, 74, 106)

- Multiples of 3: the sum of the digits is divisible by 3. ($87 = 8 + 7 = 15$; $15 \div 3 = 5$)

- Multiples of 4: the last two digits are divisible by 4. (412; $12 \div 4 = 3$)

- Multiples of 5: the last digit is 5 or 0. (285, 4110)

- Multiples of 6: the sum of the digits is divisible by 3. ($258 = 2 + 5 + 8 = 15$; $15 \div 3 = 5$)

- Multiples of 7: there are no tricks! You will just have to divide the number by 7 to find out.

- Multiples of 8: half the number is divisible by 4. ($320 \div 2 = 160$; $160 \div 4 = 40$)

- Multiples of 9: the sum of the digits is divisible by 9. ($468 = 4 + 6 + 8 = 18$; $18 \div 9 = 2$)

- Multiples of 10: the last digit is a zero. (60, 100, 2000)

Use Charlie's tips to answer these questions, Yes or No.

⑪ Is 269 a multiple of 4? ____

⑫ Is 425 a multiple of 5? ____

⑬ Is 921 a multiple of 3? ____

⑭ Is 622 a multiple of 6? ____

⑮ Is 287 a multiple of 7? ____

⑯ Is 648 a multiple of 8? ____

⑰ Is 399 a multiple of 10? ____

⑱ Is 891 a multiple of 9? ____

⑲ Is 3824 a multiple of 6? ____

⑳ Is 10 245 a multiple of 9? ____

Have a go

Some multiples of both 3 and 4 are 12 and 24. Investigate multiples of 4 and 5. How many can you find?

7: Prime numbers

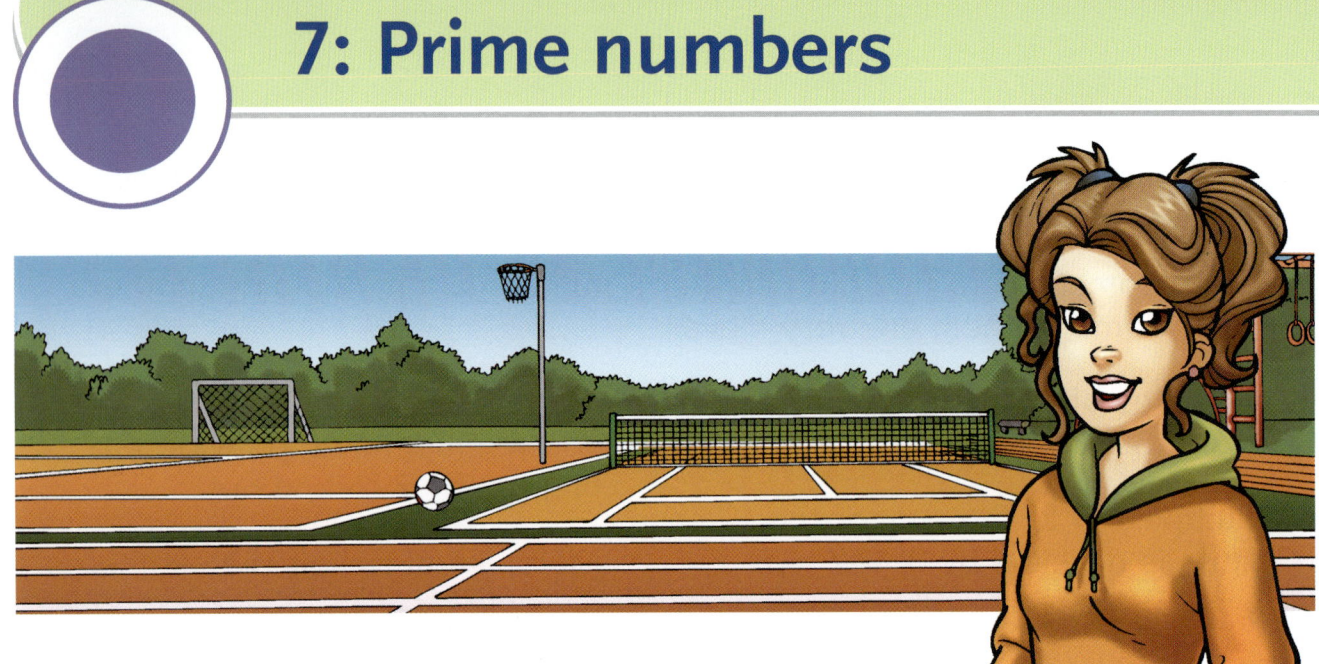

I love prime numbers! There is something very special about them.
A prime number is a number which can only be divided by itself and one.
Unusually in Maths, new prime numbers are still being discovered.
In fact, if you discover a new one you could win a prize.

Learn more about them and see what you could win at the end of the opposite page!

 **Get ready**

1. The first five prime numbers are 2, 3, 5, 7 and 11. Colour them in on this 100 square.

2. There are twenty more prime numbers under 100. Colour them in on the 100 square.

1	2	3	4	5	6	7	8	9	10
11	12	13	14	15	16	17	18	19	20
21	22	23	24	25	26	27	28	29	30
31	32	33	34	35	36	37	38	39	40
41	42	43	44	45	46	47	48	49	50
51	52	53	54	55	56	57	58	59	60
61	62	63	64	65	66	67	68	69	70
71	72	73	74	75	76	77	78	79	80
81	82	83	84	85	86	87	88	89	90
91	92	93	94	95	96	97	98	99	100

Let's practise

Around 250 years ago a mathematician called Christian Goldbach tried adding prime numbers together. He asked himself the question:

Is every even number the sum of two primes?

He thought the answer was 'yes' but he couldn't prove it. So he came to the conclusion that every even number bigger than six is the sum of two odd primes. This is called 'Goldbach's conjecture'. Let's see how this works.

8 = 5 + 3   10 = 3 + 7 and 5 + 5   12 = 7 + 5   14 = 7 + 7 and 3 + 11

3 Continue this pattern up to 50 if you can.

_____   _____

_____   _____

_____   _____

_____   _____

_____   _____

_____   _____

Have a go

Now for that prize! The Great Internet Mersenne Prime Search (GIMPS) encourages people to use their personal computers to search for new prime numbers. An organisation called the Electronic Frontier Foundation is offering $100 000 to the person who finds the first 10-million-digit prime number. More information on how to search for that 10-million-digit prime can be found at www.mersenne.org. Good luck!

This looks hard but once you know how, it's easy. Practising this at Kids Club has really helped our Maths.

To multiply whole numbers by **10**, move the digits *one* place to the left of the decimal point.

To multiply whole numbers by **100**, move the digits *two* places to the left of the decimal point.

To multiply whole numbers by **1000**, move the digits *three* places to the left of the decimal point.

Then add zeros to fill in the spaces.

56 × 10 =   560.0

56 × 100 =   5600.0

56 × 1000 = 56 000.0

Get ready

Multiply these numbers by 10, 100 and 1000.

1   35 × 10 = _____   35 × 100 = _____   35 × 1000 = _____

2   52 × 10 = _____   52 × 100 = _____   52 × 1000 = _____

3   79 × 10 = _____   79 × 100 = _____   79 × 1000 = _____

4   93 × 10 = _____   93 × 100 = _____   93 × 1000 = _____

5   471 × 10 = _____   471 × 100 = _____   471 × 1000 = _____

Let's practise

Dividing whole numbers by 10, 100 and 1000 is the opposite of multiplying, so the digits move one, two and three places to the right.

Remember, the decimal point *never* moves, the digits do.

$480 \div 10 = 48.0$

$480 \div 100 = 4.80$

$480 \div 1000 = 0.480$

Answer these questions.

6 $55 \times 10 = $ _____

7 $160 \div 10 = $ _____

8 $630 \times $ _____ $= 6300$

9 $750 \div $ _____ $= 75$

10 $61 \times $ _____ $= 61\,000$

11 $3800 \div $ _____ $= 380$

12 $523 \times 100 = $ _____

13 $2000 \div 100 = $ _____

14   _____ $\times 100 = 2100$

15 $83 \times $ _____ $= 83\,000$

16 $45 \times 100 = $ _____

17 $4600 \div $ _____ $= 460$

18 $230 \div $ _____ $= 23$

19 $582 \times 100 = $ _____

Have a go

Do you have any savings or are you given pocket money each week? Maybe you earn money by doing jobs around the house. How much would you have if you multiplied all your money by 10, 100 or 1000?

The children at Kids Club want to learn to play tennis. First we need to learn more about fractions, decimals and percentages so we can shop for equipment and hope to get a few bargains. I saw a pair of trainers last week with a '50% off' tag on them – I didn't know what it meant.

Charlie and Abbie said they would help us.

This is a table for commonly used fraction, decimal and percentage equivalents.

Remember, 'equivalent' means 'the same as'.

Fraction	Decimal	Percentage
1 whole	1.0	100%
$\frac{3}{4}$	0.75	75%
$\frac{1}{2}$	0.50	50%
$\frac{1}{3}$	0.333	33.33%
$\frac{1}{4}$	0.25	25%
$\frac{1}{5}$	0.20	20%
$\frac{1}{10}$	0.10	10%
$\frac{1}{20}$	0.05	5%
$\frac{1}{100}$	0.01	1%

Get ready

1. Which decimal is the equivalent to 75%? _____

2. Which fraction is the equivalent to 0.20? _____

3. Which percentage is the equivalent to 0.25? _____

4. Which decimal is the equivalent to $\frac{1}{20}$? _____

5. Which fraction is the equivalent to 1%? _____

6. Which percentage is the equivalent to 1 whole? _____

 ## Let's practise

Our knowledge of fraction, decimal and percentage equivalents can help us work out other problems.

25% of 40 is the same as $\frac{1}{4}$ of 40, which is 10.

So, if the trainers were priced at £20 and had a ticket on saying '50% off', the new price would be £10.

$50\% = \frac{1}{2}$
$\frac{1}{2}$ of £20 = £10

Use the table to help you answer these questions.

7 If the price of a tennis racquet is £30, how much would it be with 50% off? _____

8 A new tennis shirt costs £16. In a sale, the price is reduced by a quarter. How much is the shirt in the sale? _____

9 A box of tennis balls was priced at £12. The manager reduced the price by 75%. How much did they cost then? _____

10 A shop assistant priced a pair of shorts at £10. They should have cost a fifth more than this. How much was this? _____

11 A tennis coach offered a series of tennis lessons for £80. Nobody took up the offer, so the coach reduced the price by 10%. What was the new price of the tennis lessons? _____

 ## Have a go

Next time you are out shopping, look for items in a sale or being sold with promises of percentage discounts. Look at the original price and the price after the discount. Which ones look like bargains?

As well as using our knowledge of equivalents we also need to be able to find fractions using division. We do this by dividing by the denominator.

$\frac{1}{4}$ of 36p = 36 ÷ 4 = 9

Now let's look at finding a percentage of a total.
Three months ago, Alfie broke our TV when he was practising his skateboard skills – indoors.

Charlie has seen a TV which costs £260. It is now in the sale with 65% off. What is the new price after the discount?

Well, 50% off is half = £130
Another 10% off is £26 so = £130 – £26 = £104
And another 5% off is £13 (half of £26) so = £104 – £13 = £91

Get ready

Find the prices of these items after the discount.

1 30% off a bike costing £50 _____

2 10% off an MP3 player costing £75 _____

3 15% off a DVD costing £20 _____

4 45% off a lap-top costing £200 _____

5 75% off a console game costing £30 _____

Let's practise

Now let's look at finding some harder fractions of totals.

For example, $\frac{5}{8}$ of 96 CDs.
First find $\frac{1}{8}$, $96 \div 8 = 12$
So, $\frac{5}{8}$ is $5 \times 12 = 60$

Now find the fractions of these totals.

6 $\frac{3}{4}$ of 48 books _____

7 $\frac{3}{5}$ of 75 chocolates _____

8 $\frac{6}{7}$ of 63 apples _____

9 $\frac{2}{3}$ of 72 magazines _____

10 $\frac{5}{6}$ of 240 stickers _____

11 $\frac{3}{8}$ of 136 cakes _____

12   Which is less and by how much: $\frac{4}{5}$ of £135 or $\frac{8}{9}$ of £135?

_____

Have a go

You can use a calculator to turn a fraction into a percentage.
If you scored $\frac{78}{120}$ in a spelling test, you could work out what that score would be as a percentage.
Key in 78, then the divide key, then 120, and then the % key.
Your calculator should read 65, so 78 out of 120 is 65%.
Practise changing your marks at school into percentages.

11: More about fractions

Fractions have given children like us headaches for years! We have worked really hard at Kids Club so we can show you some information which might help you – and not give you a headache.

Improper fractions
These are fractions which are bigger than one.
$\frac{8}{5}$ is an improper fraction. It can be written as $1\frac{3}{5}$.

Simplifying fractions
Simplifying fractions to their lowest form means cancelling their common factors.
Look at this fraction: $\frac{12}{36}$.
Both the **top (numerator)** and the **bottom (denominator)** can be divided by 12; $12 \div 12 = 1$ and $36 \div 12 = 3$, so the simplest form of $\frac{12}{36}$ is $\frac{1}{3}$.

Common denominators
We can add fractions with different denominators by finding a common denominator. Look at $\frac{2}{3} + \frac{3}{4}$. The lowest number that both denominators can divide into is 12.
So the fractions are changed into twelfths. Remember, whatever you multiply the denominator by, you must do the same for the numerator.

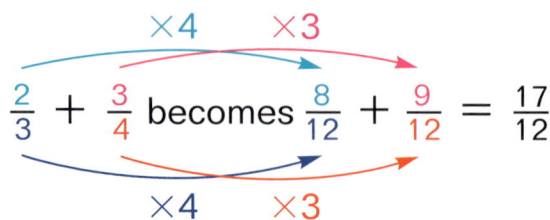

$\frac{2}{3} + \frac{3}{4}$ becomes $\frac{8}{12} + \frac{9}{12} = \frac{17}{12}$

$\frac{17}{12}$ is an improper fraction and can be written as $1\frac{5}{12}$.

Get ready

Write these improper fractions as mixed numbers.

1 $\frac{5}{4}$ _____

2 $\frac{7}{5}$ _____

3 $\frac{8}{3}$ _____

4 $\frac{9}{5}$ _____

5 $\frac{10}{7}$ _____

 ## Let's practise

Simplify these fractions to their lowest form.

6　$\frac{20}{60}$ _____

7　$\frac{21}{42}$ _____

8　$\frac{48}{64}$ _____

9　$\frac{32}{128}$ _____

10　$\frac{56}{88}$ _____

Convert these pairs of fractions so they have the lowest common denominator, then add them together.

11　$\frac{1}{5}$ and $\frac{1}{6}$　_____ and _____ = _____

12　$\frac{1}{4}$ and $\frac{2}{5}$　_____ and _____ = _____

13　$\frac{5}{6}$ and $\frac{1}{8}$　_____ and _____ = _____

14　$\frac{3}{7}$ and $\frac{1}{4}$　_____ and _____ = _____

Have a go

Have you noticed how tricky it can be to cut a pizza or cake into equal pieces? If you cut it into halves or quarters it's quite easy, but what about into thirds or fifths?

Draw some circles on paper and practise dividing them into equal thirds, fifths, sixths, sevenths, eighths, ninths and tenths.

Practise, then amaze your friends with your new found pizza skills!

Last week we held an outdoor fair and barbeque to raise money to buy some outdoor adventure equipment. It was a great success – even if the sausages that Alfie cooked were black on the outside and frozen in the middle!

The equipment is really cool but it costs £1599!

I have been given the task of adding up the money to see if we have raised enough.

I'm going to need your help.

Get ready

These are the sums we raised on the different stalls and from the barbeque.

Add these totals.

1
```
    £42.67
 +  £15.83
 ─────────
 ─────────
```

3
```
    £30.22
 +  £89.97
 ─────────
 ─────────
```

5
```
    £83.34
 +  £26.99
 ─────────
 ─────────
```

2
```
    £61.57
 +  £48.29
 ─────────
 ─────────
```

4
```
    £11.70
 +  £16.44
 ─────────
 ─────────
```

What is the total amount of money raised? _____

How much more do we need for the outdoor equipment? _____

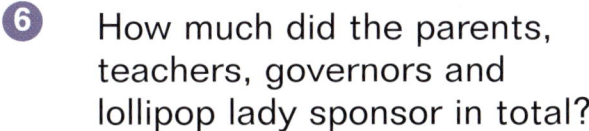

Let's practise

To raise the extra money, Charlie and Abbie did a sponsored parachute jump!

Look at their list of sponsors in the table.

6 How much did the parents, teachers, governors and lollipop lady sponsor in total?

_____

7 What is the difference between the amounts the teaching assistants and the governors sponsored? _____

8 How much did the bank, mayor, restaurant and local businessman sponsor in total?

_____

Sponsor	Amount
Kids' parents	£306.50
School teachers	£252.78
Friends	£189.41
School governors	£92.67
The local bank	£100
The teaching assistants	£210.69
A local businessman	£50
A local restaurant	£87.95
The mayor	£10
The lollipop lady	£50

9 What was the total amount of money raised from the parachute jump?

_____

10 How much money was left once the outdoor equipment had been bought? _____

Have a go

You could ask friends and family to sponsor you. Raise money for a local cause by doing something like swimming or running or something unusual like staying silent for a whole day! Best to leave the parachuting to adults though . . .

13: Ordering decimals

I've been revising some Maths at Kids Club. I keep getting mixed up with decimal numbers. As ever, Charlie and Abbie have really helped me! This is what we did.

Decimals are not whole numbers. For example, the decimal 4.8 is 'in between' 4 and 5. We say it as '4 point 8'. Look at 4.8 on this number line.

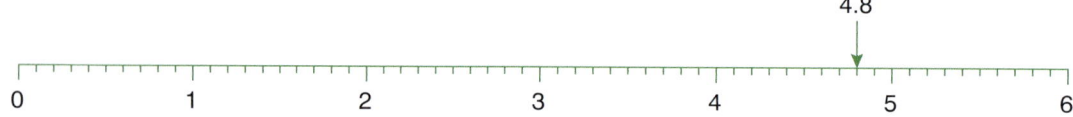

Get ready

Mark an arrow at the correct place to show each number on these number lines.

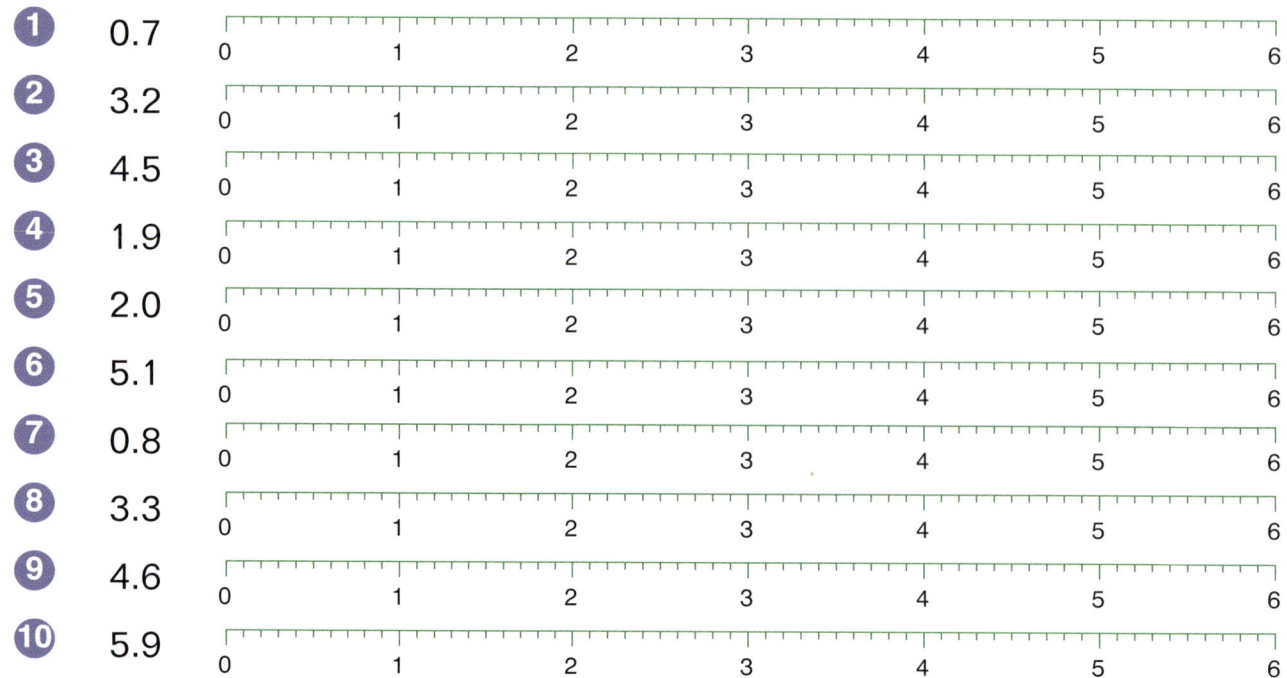

1. 0.7
2. 3.2
3. 4.5
4. 1.9
5. 2.0
6. 5.1
7. 0.8
8. 3.3
9. 4.6
10. 5.9

**Let's practise**

Amina:	2.51 m
Kim:	3.28 m
Alfie:	2.79 m
Jamelia:	3.72 m
Megan:	2.89 m

These are the results from our school sports day long jump competition.

11 Write the distances down in order of size, starting with the longest jump.   1st _____ 2nd _____
3rd _____ 4th _____ 5th _____

12 These are the results from the javelin competition.

Amina:	23.72 m
Kim:	15.29 m
Alfie:	23.78 m
Jamelia:	18.33 m
Megan:	15.38 m

Write the distances down in order of size, starting with the furthest throw.
1st _____ 2nd _____ 3rd _____
4th _____ 5th _____

Now practise by putting these decimals in order. Start with the smallest number.

13 0.42, 0.31, 1.82, 0.57 _____

14 23.32, 32.21, 33.45, 22.31 _____

15 0.414, 0.441, 0.431, 0.042 _____

**Have a go**

Look in the sports results section of a newspaper. Find the results for an athletics event or a sport which measures distance. Write down as many decimals as you can on separate pieces of paper. Mix them up and order them by size. Be careful not to choose timed events because these are not measured using the decimal system.

I had trouble multiplying and dividing decimals at school. Abbie showed me that by using my knowledge of place value and multiplication facts, I could calculate them really easily. And no, I didn't need a calculator! This is what she told me.

Look at this question: 0.8×7

If we ignore the decimal point and look at the digits, I can use my times tables to do the calculation: $8 \times 7 = 56$

Now I need to replace the decimal point. I can use my knowledge of place value to decide where to put it.

0.56, 5.6 or 56.0?

I know that 0.8 is a little less than 1, so $0.8 \times 7 = 5.6$

I'm correct!

Get ready

Use your knowledge of multiplication facts and place value to answer these.

1 0.3×5 _____

2 0.8×4 _____

3 0.7×6 _____

4 0.9×3 _____

5 0.4×7 _____

6 1.0×5 _____

7 1.0×9 _____

8 0.5×10 _____

9 0.2×2 _____

10 0.1×1 _____

Let's practise

Now use your knowledge of multiplication and division facts to answer these.

⑪   4.8 ÷ 6 _____

⑫   2.1 ÷ 7 _____

⑬   5.6 ÷ 8 _____

⑭   3.2 ÷ 4 _____

⑮   8.1 ÷ 9 _____

⑯   2.8 ÷ 7 _____

⑰   7.2 ÷ 9 _____

⑱   6.4 ÷ 8 _____

⑲   4.9 ÷ 7 _____

⑳   2.7 ÷ 3 _____

Have a go

Learning your 'tables' is very important for all areas of Maths.

They are like a 'mental tool box' which you carry around in your head to fix Maths problems.

When you have learnt them thoroughly, practise with a friend, answering questions at speed. How fast can you answer? Try to beat your record.

I rushed a Maths test at school last week and finished first. I thought I'd done really well, but when I got my paper back I was disappointed. I'd made so many silly mistakes!

Charlie told me that I must always check my answers.

Here are two ways to do that.

Inverse operations
Remember, addition and subtraction are opposites.
Multiplication and division are also opposites.
We can use this knowledge to check our answers.

$56 + 24 = 80$ so $80 - 24 = 56$
$33 \times 5 = 165$ so $165 \div 5 = 33$

Approximating by rounding
Another way to check your answers is by rounding the numbers in the question up or down to the nearest 10, 100 or 1000. You can then use your knowledge of multiplication, addition, subtraction and division facts to give you a rough answer.

$387 + 512$ is roughly $400 + 500 = 900$
47×22 is roughly $50 \times 20 = 1000$

If your rough answer is fairly close to your original calculation then you know your answer should be correct. If not, check your rough answer and then your calculation.

Do these calculations, then check the answers using the inverse method.

1 $537 - 83 =$ _____   Check: _____ $+ 83 =$ _____

2 $160 \div 4 =$ _____   Check: _____ $\times 4 =$ _____

3 $843 + 585 =$ _____   Check: _____ $- 585 =$ _____

4 $37 \times 5 =$ _____   Check: _____ $\div 5 =$ _____

Let's practise

Give estimates to the nearest 10, 100 or 1000 for these questions.

Write the calculation, then the answer.

The first one has been done for you.

5 104 × 28 = 100 × 30 = 3000

6 396 ÷ 18 = _____

7 310 + 993 = _____

8 884 − 285 = _____

9 417 × 48 = _____

10 312 ÷ 52 = _____

11 297 + 809 = _____

12 606 − 111 = _____

Use a calculator or a paper and pencil method to get exact answers to the calculations. Were your estimates close? Were any exact?

Have a go

Large distances or measures are often given as approximate figures.

The Sun is approximately 93 million miles from the Earth.

Use books and the Internet to find these approximate measures:

- the distance to the Moon
- the distance to Jupiter
- the population of the United Kingdom
- the population of India.

16: Using a calculator

The pocket calculator is often seen as the answer to all Maths problems.

Alfie used one for his Maths homework last week but got every question wrong. He blamed the calculator! They are only useful if you use them correctly.

Here are some tips on using a calculator successfully.

- Does the question need a calculator? Can you do the sum in your head?
- Would using a written method be easier or quicker?
- Whatever the calculation, make an estimate first. Is the answer on the calculator screen close to your estimate?
- Always check the screen to check you have pressed the right keys.
- Don't forget to press the decimal point key when entering decimal numbers.
- If you make a mistake, cancel the operation and start again.
- Think clearly – say the calculation in your head as you press the keys.

Get ready

Use a calculator to answer these questions. Think which signs to use!

1   37 × _____ = 111

2   245 – _____ = 150

3   _____ ÷ 7 = 56

4   There are 5 players in a chess team. There are 18 chess teams in a league. How many players are there in the league? _____

5   Write down what the three missing digits could be in this calculation.
_____ _____ × _____ = 588

Use a calculator to tackle these problems.

6 250 000 children joined some form
of after-school club last year.
40% of the children joined in September.
15% of the children joined in December.

How many children joined in the rest of the year? _____

7 Kim, Megan and Alfie each stand for a whole number.

They add together to make 1500.
Kim + Megan + Alfie = 1500
Megan is three times as big as Alfie.
Kim is twice as big as Alfie.
Calculate the value of Kim, Megan and Alfie.

Kim = _____, Megan = _____, Alfie = _____

Have a go

Did you know your pocket calculator can write?
Type . (decimal point) 7734 into your calculator.
Turn it upside down. What does it say?
Experiment with your 'calculator alphabet'.
What other words or phrases can you write?

Whenever you approach a calculation, the first thing you should ask yourself is 'can I do it in my head?' Often the answer will be 'yes'. If the calculation is too difficult then you need to use a reliable written method.

Here are examples of written methods for all four operations that you will be, or have been, taught at school.

Addition

466 + 558
Estimate: 500 + 600 = 1100

```
   466
 + 558
 ------
  1024
 ------
  1 1 1
```

The 'carry' digits are recorded below the line.

Subtraction

603 − 378
Estimate: 600 − 400 = 200

```
   5 9 13
   6̸0̸3̸
 − 378
 ------
   225
 ------
```

Multiplication

58 × 29
Estimate: 60 × 30 = 1800

```
    58
 ×  29
 ------
   522    (58 × 9)
 ------
  1160    (58 × 20)
 ------
  1682
 ------
```

Division

560 ÷ 24
Estimate: 600 ÷ 25 = 24

$$24\overline{)\,56_80}\quad 23\ r8$$

Let's practise

Now it's time to practise the written methods so you'll get the answer correct every time. Use extra paper for your workings.

Remember to estimate first by mental calculation using the rounding method.

1 875 + 976 = _____

2 692 + 933 = _____

3 494 + 778 = _____

4 731 − 469 = _____

5 844 − 327 = _____

6 503 − 224 = _____

7 83 × 34 = _____

8 75 × 69 = _____

9 82 × 87 = _____

10 782 ÷ 16 = _____

11 874 ÷ 28 = _____

12 675 ÷ 27 = _____

Have a go

For all calculations, think:

• Can I do it in my head?
• If not, can I use a written method?
• If the calculation is too hard, use a calculator.

Remember: estimate, calculate, check.

How have I done?

Now it's time to see what you have learnt at Kids Club.
Have a go at these questions.

1 What is the value of the highlighted digit? £56**2**.45 (1 mark) _____

2 Write an equivalent fraction for a) $\frac{1}{4}$ _____ b) $\frac{1}{3}$ _____
c) $\frac{4}{10}$ _____ (3 marks)

3 What percentage of this grid is coloured
in? (1 mark) _____

4 If 12 eggs feed 8 people, how many eggs
would you need to feed 12 people?
(1 mark) _____

5 What is £75.50 a) doubled? _____
b) halved? _____ (1 mark)

6 Write down the factors of 18.
(1 mark) _____

7 Which of these is a multiple of 9? 4723, 4724, 4725, 4726 (1 mark)
_____

8 Which of these is a prime number? 50, 51, 52, 53 (1 mark)
_____

9 Fill in the missing numbers. a) 10 × ? = 560 _____
b) ? ÷ 100 = 8 _____ c) 42 × ? = 42 000 _____ (3 marks)

10 What is the decimal equivalent of a) $\frac{1}{4}$? _____
b) 75%? _____ (2 marks)

11 What is 60% of £320? (1 mark) _____

12 What is $\frac{3}{5}$ of 80? (1 mark) _____

13 What is the total of 43.87 and 21.39? (1 mark) _____

14 Put these decimals in order, highest first. 0.1, 0.71, 0.17, 7.01, 0.07
(1 mark)_____

15 Multiply these decimals. a) $1.4 \times 5 =$ _____
b) $3.7 \times 3 =$ _____ (2 marks)

16 Divide these decimals. a) $4.8 \div 12 =$ _____
b) $7.2 \div 6 =$ _____ (2 marks)

17 Estimate an answer for this calculation. 89×11 (1 mark)

_____

18 Check this calculation: $846 \div 6 = 139$. Right or wrong? (1 mark)

_____

19 Which is worth more, a million pounds or £1 doubled 20 times? Use a
calculator to work out the answer. (1 mark)

_____

20 Use a written method to calculate these. a) $593 + 478 =$ _____
b) $735 - 369 =$ _____ c) $82 \times 43 =$ _____ d) $504 \div 14 =$ _____
(4 marks)

Total marks: $\frac{}{30}$

We hope you have learnt a lot and
enjoyed your stay at Kids Club.
See you soon!

Maths tools

These may help you with some of the questions in this book.

1 WHOLE									

Fraction blocks showing:

- $\frac{1}{2}$ $\frac{1}{2}$
- $\frac{1}{3}$ $\frac{1}{3}$ $\frac{1}{3}$
- $\frac{1}{4}$ $\frac{1}{4}$ $\frac{1}{4}$ $\frac{1}{4}$
- $\frac{1}{5}$ $\frac{1}{5}$ $\frac{1}{5}$ $\frac{1}{5}$ $\frac{1}{5}$
- $\frac{1}{6}$ $\frac{1}{6}$ $\frac{1}{6}$ $\frac{1}{6}$ $\frac{1}{6}$ $\frac{1}{6}$
- $\frac{1}{7}$ $\frac{1}{7}$ $\frac{1}{7}$ $\frac{1}{7}$ $\frac{1}{7}$ $\frac{1}{7}$ $\frac{1}{7}$
- $\frac{1}{8}$ $\frac{1}{8}$ $\frac{1}{8}$ $\frac{1}{8}$ $\frac{1}{8}$ $\frac{1}{8}$ $\frac{1}{8}$ $\frac{1}{8}$
- $\frac{1}{9}$ $\frac{1}{9}$ $\frac{1}{9}$ $\frac{1}{9}$ $\frac{1}{9}$ $\frac{1}{9}$ $\frac{1}{9}$ $\frac{1}{9}$ $\frac{1}{9}$
- $\frac{1}{10}$ $\frac{1}{10}$ $\frac{1}{10}$ $\frac{1}{10}$ $\frac{1}{10}$ $\frac{1}{10}$ $\frac{1}{10}$ $\frac{1}{10}$ $\frac{1}{10}$ $\frac{1}{10}$

Fraction, decimal and percentage equivalents

$\frac{1}{2} = 0.50 = 50\%$

$\frac{1}{4} = 0.25 = 25\%$

$\frac{3}{4} = 0.75 = 75\%$

$\frac{1}{10} = 0.10 = 10\%$

$\frac{1}{100} = 0.01 = 1\%$

$\frac{1}{3} = 0.333 = 33.33\%$

1 whole = 1.0 = 100%

$\frac{1}{3} = 0.33 = 33\%$ (approximately)

$\frac{2}{3} = 0.66 = 66\%$ (approximately)

1	2	3	4	5	6	7	8	9	10
11	12	13	14	15	16	17	18	19	20
21	22	23	24	25	26	27	28	29	30
31	32	33	34	35	36	37	38	39	40
41	42	43	44	45	46	47	48	49	50
51	52	53	54	55	56	57	58	59	60
61	62	63	64	65	66	67	68	69	70
71	72	73	74	75	76	77	78	79	80
81	82	83	84	85	86	87	88	89	90
91	92	93	94	95	96	97	98	99	100

Use this hundred square to help you with your calculations.

Multiplication tables

1 x 1 = 1	2 x 1 = 2	3 x 1 = 3	4 x 1 = 4	5 x 1 = 5	6 x 1 = 6
1 x 2 = 2	2 x 2 = 4	3 x 2 = 6	4 x 2 = 8	5 x 2 = 10	6 x 2 = 12
1 x 3 = 3	2 x 3 = 6	3 x 3 = 9	4 x 3 = 12	5 x 3 = 15	6 x 3 = 18
1 x 4 = 4	2 x 4 = 8	3 x 4 = 12	4 x 4 = 16	5 x 4 = 20	6 x 4 = 24
1 x 5 = 5	2 x 5 = 10	3 x 5 = 15	4 x 5 = 20	5 x 5 = 25	6 x 5 = 30
1 x 6 = 6	2 x 6 = 12	3 x 6 = 18	4 x 6 = 24	5 x 6 = 30	6 x 6 = 36
1 x 7 = 7	2 x 7 = 14	3 x 7 = 21	4 x 7 = 28	5 x 7 = 35	6 x 7 = 42
1 x 8 = 8	2 x 8 = 16	3 x 8 = 24	4 x 8 = 32	5 x 8 = 40	6 x 8 = 48
1 x 9 = 9	2 x 9 = 18	3 x 9 = 27	4 x 9 = 36	5 x 9 = 45	6 x 9 = 54
1 x 10 = 10	2 x 10 = 20	3 x 10 = 30	4 x 10 = 40	5 x 10 = 50	6 x 10 = 60
1 x 11 = 11	2 x 11 = 22	3 x 11 = 33	4 x 11 = 44	5 x 11 = 55	6 x 11 = 66
1 x 12 = 12	2 x 12 = 24	3 x 12 = 36	4 x 12 = 48	5 x 12 = 60	6 x 12 = 72

7 x 1 = 7	8 x 1 = 8	9 x 1 = 9	10 x 1 = 10	11 x 1 = 11	12 x 1 = 12
7 x 2 = 14	8 x 2 = 16	9 x 2 = 18	10 x 2 = 20	11 x 2 = 22	12 x 2 = 24
7 x 3 = 21	8 x 3 = 24	9 x 3 = 27	10 x 3 = 30	11 x 3 = 33	12 x 3 = 36
7 x 4 = 28	8 x 4 = 32	9 x 4 = 36	10 x 4 = 40	11 x 4 = 44	12 x 4 = 48
7 x 5 = 35	8 x 5 = 40	9 x 5 = 45	10 x 5 = 50	11 x 5 = 55	12 x 5 = 60
7 x 6 = 42	8 x 6 = 48	9 x 6 = 54	10 x 6 = 60	11 x 6 = 66	12 x 6 = 72
7 x 7 = 49	8 x 7 = 56	9 x 7 = 63	10 x 7 = 70	11 x 7 = 77	12 x 7 = 84
7 x 8 = 56	8 x 8 = 64	9 x 8 = 72	10 x 8 = 80	11 x 8 = 88	12 x 8 = 96
7 x 9 = 63	8 x 9 = 72	9 x 9 = 81	10 x 9 = 90	11 x 9 = 99	12 x 9 = 108
7 x 10 = 70	8 x 10 = 80	9 x 10 = 90	10 x 10 = 100	11 x 10 = 110	12 x 10 = 120
7 x 11 = 77	8 x 11 = 88	9 x 11 = 99	10 x 11 = 110	11 x 11 = 121	12 x 11 = 132
7 x 12 = 84	8 x 12 = 96	9 x 12 = 108	10 x 12 = 120	11 x 12 = 132	12 x 12 = 144

Number line from –20 to +20

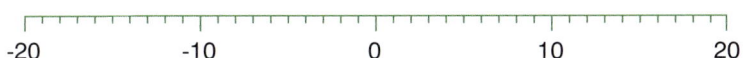

-20   -10   0   10   20

Glossary

This glossary offers the definitions of 22 important mathematical terms to do with number and calculation which you are introduced to in Years 5 and 6. There are many others to learn but these make a good starting point. Try learning the correct spellings as well as what the words mean.

Addition vocabulary – These words and phrases all relate to 'addition': add, altogether, find the sum of, how many more, plus, increase, total.

Clear – Clear the screen of a calculator by pressing the 'C' button (clear) or 'AC' button (all clear).

Currency – The money that is used in a particular country at a particular time. The currency of the United Kingdom is the pound (£).

Decimal place – The position of a number after a decimal point (.) The number 5.279 is expressed to three decimal places.

Denominator – The number below the line in a fraction. In $\frac{1}{2}$, the denominator is 2.

Digit – 0, 1, 2, 3, 4, 5, 6, 7, 8 and 9 are all digits. They become numbers when they are given a 'place value'.

Division vocabulary – These words and phrases all relate to 'division': share, share equally, equal groups of, divided by, divided into, divisible by, factor.

Equivalent – 'The same as'. So 50% is the same as $\frac{1}{2}$ and 0.5.

Factor – A number which exactly divides into another number.

Formula – An accepted way of doing something; a mathematical rule expressed in a set of numbers and letters. 'The area of a rectangle = length $\times$ breadth or 'area = l $\times$ b'.

Fraction – A number that results from one whole number being divided by another; a small part of something.

Inverse – The opposite of something. The inverse of addition is subtraction. The inverse of multiplication is division.

Multiple – A number that may be divided by another number without a remainder.

Multiplication vocabulary – These words and phrases all relate to 'multiplication': lots of, groups of, times, multiply, multiplied by, multiple of, product, once, twice, three times . . . ten times . . .

Numerator – The number above the line in a fraction. In $\frac{1}{4}$, the numerator is 1.

Percentage – A fraction expressed as part of 100.

Prime factor – Any factor of a number that is a prime number.

Prime number – A whole number greater than 1 which is only divisible by itself and 1. The first five prime numbers are 2, 3, 5, 7, 11.

Recurring decimal – A decimal fraction with an infinite (never-ending) repeating digit or group of digits. $\frac{1}{3}$ as a decimal fraction is 0.3333333.

Sequence – A succession of terms formed according to a rule. The famous Fibonacci sequence is formed by adding the two previous numbers to form the next number in the sequence – 0, 1, 1, 2, 3, 5, 8, 13, 21, etc.

Square number – A number that is the product of two equal numbers. 49 is a square number ($7 \times 7 = 49$).

Subtraction vocabulary – These words and phrases all relate to 'subtraction': subtract, take, take away, minus, decrease, leave, how many are left, how many are left over, find the difference between, half, halve, how many fewer is . . . than . . . ?

Answers

Unit 1 (pages 6 and 7)
1 8 pounds and 65 pence
2 22 pounds and 41 pence
3 61 pounds and 77 pence
4 89 pounds and 88 pence
5 107 pounds and 90 pence
6 225 pounds and 51 pence
7 312 pounds and 21 pence
8 199 pounds and 99 pence
9 88 pounds and 8 pence
10 501 pounds and 75 pence
11 £20 + £1 + 80p + 9p rounded to £22
12 £10 + £3 + 70p + 5p rounded to £14
13 £50 + £2 + 80p + 8p rounded to £53
14 £70 + £2 + 70p + 1p rounded to £73
15 £90 + £4 + 20p + 6p rounded to £94
16 £80 + £1 + 40p + 5p rounded to £81
17 £30 + £5 + 90p + 4p rounded to £36
18 £60 + £8 + 10p + 0p rounded to £68
19 £40 + £9 + 50p + 7p rounded to £50
20 £10 + £1 + 30p + 3p rounded to £11

Unit 2 (pages 8 and 9)
1 $\frac{2}{4}$
2 $\frac{3}{6}$
3 $\frac{4}{8}$
4 $\frac{5}{10}$
5 $\frac{2}{6}$ and $\frac{3}{9}$
6 $\frac{1}{4}$
7 $\frac{4}{10}$
8 $\frac{4}{6}$ and $\frac{6}{9}$
9 $\frac{3}{4}$
10 The sevenths

Unit 3 (pages 10 and 11)
1 60%
2 75%
3 30%
4 25%
5 40%
6 5%
7 15%
8 95%
9 50%
10 10%
11 10%
12 18%
13 25%
14 32%
15 50%
16 64%
17 75%
18 86%

Unit 4 (pages 12 and 13)
1 24 trifle sponges
   16 cups of whipped cream
   16 cups of custard
   8 cans of fruit cocktail
   32 glacé cherries
2 6 trifle sponges
   4 cups of whipped cream
   4 cups of custard
   2 cans of fruit cocktail
   8 glacé cherries
3 3.2 kg of chicken
   600 ml of chicken stock
   8 carrots
   4 onions
   100 g of butter
   160 g of plain flour
   Cooking time = 2 hours and 40 minutes

Unit 5 (pages 14 and 15)
1 6.8
2 8.4
3 3.6
4 5.0
5 10.0
6 1.1
7 2.4
8 1.8
9 2.7
10 3.1
11 £2.50
12 £4.60
13 £6.86
14 £10.36
15 £8.48
16 £3.22
17 £4.30
18 £5.13
19 £2.41
20 a) £33.40 b) £8.35

Unit 6 (pages 16 and 17)
1 1, 2, 4
2 1, 2, 4, 8
3 1, 2, 4, 8, 16
4 1, 2, 4, 5, 10, 20
5 1, 2, 4, 8, 16, 32
6 1, 2, 4, 8, 16, 32, 64
7 1, 2, 19, 38
8 1, 2, 3, 6, 7, 14, 21, 42
9 1, 2, 4, 7, 8, 14, 28, 56
10 1, 2, 4, 5, 10, 20, 25, 50, 100
11 No
12 Yes
13 Yes
14 No
15 Yes
16 Yes
17 No
18 Yes
19 No
20 No

Unit 7 (pages 18 and 19)

1, 2 The prime numbers up to 100 are 2, 3, 5, 7, 11, 13, 17, 19, 23, 29, 31, 37, 41, 43, 47, 53, 59, 61, 67, 71, 73, 79, 83, 89, 97

3 Goldbach's conjecture up to 50:

$16 = 13 + 3$ and $11 + 5$

$18 = 7 + 11$ and $5 + 13$

$20 = 3 + 17$ and $7 + 13$

$22 = 3 + 19$ and $11 + 11$ and $5 + 17$

$24 = 5 + 19$ and $7 + 17$ and $11 + 13$

$26 = 3 + 23$ and $7 + 19$ and $13 + 13$

$28 = 5 + 23$ and $11 + 17$

$30 = 7 + 23$ and $11 + 19$ and $13 + 17$

$32 = 3 + 29$ and $13 + 19$

$34 = 3 + 31$ and $5 + 29$ and $11 + 23$ and $17 + 17$

$36 = 5 + 31$ and $7 + 29$ and $13 + 23$ and $17 + 19$

$38 = 7 + 31$ and $19 + 19$

$40 = 3 + 37$ and $11 + 29$ and $17 + 23$

$42 = 5 + 37$ and $11 + 31$ and $13 + 29$ and $19 + 23$

$44 = 3 + 41$ and $7 + 37$ and $13 + 31$

$46 = 3 + 43$ and $5 + 41$ and $17 + 29$ and $23 + 23$

$48 = 5 + 43$ and $7 + 41$ and $11 + 37$ and $17 + 31$ and $19 + 29$

$50 = 3 + 47$ and $7 + 43$ and $13 + 37$ and $19 + 31$

Unit 8 (pages 20 and 21)

1 350, 3500, 35 000
2 520, 5200, 52 000
3 790, 7900, 79 000
4 930, 9300, 93 000
5 4710, 47 100, 471 000
6 550
7 16
8 10
9 10
10 1000
11 10
12 52 300
13 20
14 21
15 1000
16 4500
17 10
18 10
19 58 200

Unit 9 (pages 22 and 23)

1 0.75
2 $\frac{1}{5}$
3 25%
4 0.05
5 $\frac{1}{100}$
6 100%
7 £15
8 £12
9 £3
10 £12
11 £72

Unit 10 (pages 24 and 25)

1 £35
2 £67.50
3 £17
4 £110
5 £7.50
6 36
7 45
8 54
9 48
10 200
11 51
12 $\frac{4}{5}$, by £12

Unit 11 (pages 26 and 27)

1 $1\frac{1}{4}$
2 $1\frac{2}{5}$
3 $2\frac{2}{3}$
4 $1\frac{4}{5}$
5 $1\frac{3}{7}$
6 $\frac{1}{3}$
7 $\frac{1}{2}$
8 $\frac{3}{4}$
9 $\frac{1}{4}$
10 $\frac{7}{11}$
11 $\frac{6}{30}$ and $\frac{5}{30} = \frac{11}{30}$
12 $\frac{5}{20}$ and $\frac{8}{20} = \frac{13}{20}$
13 $\frac{20}{24}$ and $\frac{3}{24} = \frac{23}{24}$
14 $\frac{12}{28}$ and $\frac{7}{28} = \frac{19}{28}$

Unit 12 (pages 28 and 29)

1 £58.50
2 £109.86
3 £120.19
4 £28.14
5 £110.33
6 £701.95
7 £118.02
8 £247.95
9 £1350
10 £178.02
Total = £427.02;
£1171.98 still needed

Unit 13 (pages 30 and 31)

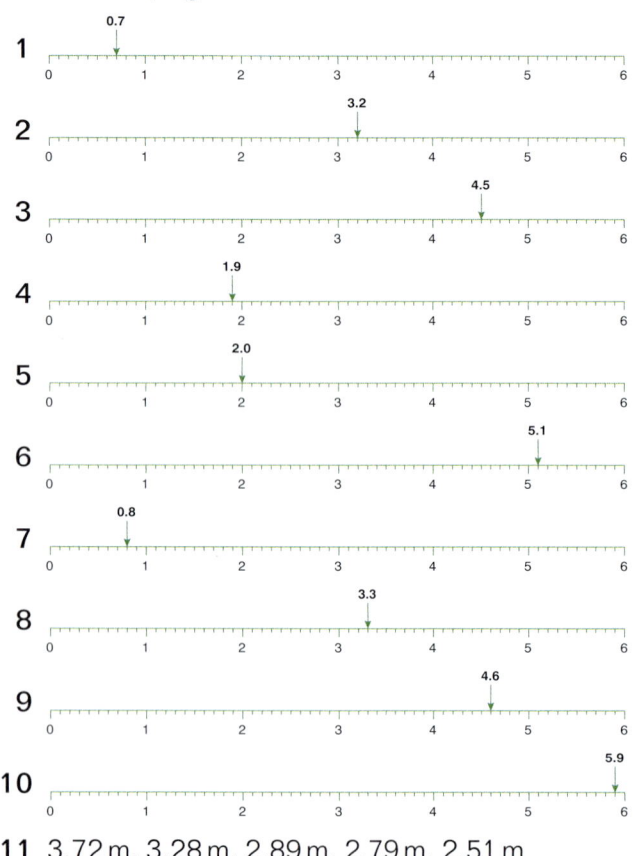

1. (0.7)
2. (3.2)
3. (4.5)
4. (1.9)
5. (2.0)
6. (5.1)
7. (0.8)
8. (3.3)
9. (4.6)
10. (5.9)

11 3.72 m, 3.28 m, 2.89 m, 2.79 m, 2.51 m
12 23.78 m, 23.72 m, 18.33 m, 15.38 m, 15.29 m
13 0.31, 0.42, 0.57, 1.82
14 22.31, 23.32, 32.21, 33.45
15 0.042, 0.414, 0.431, 0.441

Unit 14 (pages 32 and 33)

1 1.5	8 5.0	15 0.9
2 3.2	9 0.4	16 0.4
3 4.2	10 0.1	17 0.8
4 2.7	11 0.8	18 0.8
5 2.8	12 0.3	19 0.7
6 5.0	13 0.7	20 0.9
7 9.0	14 0.8	

Unit 15 (pages 34 and 35)

1 454: 454 + 83 = 537
2 40: 40 × 4 = 160
3 1428: 1428 − 585 = 843
4 185: 185 ÷ 5 = 37
5 100 × 30 = 3000 (exact answer: 2912)
6 400 ÷ 20 = 20 (exact answer: 22)
7 300 + 1000 = 1300 (exact answer: 1303)
8 900 − 300 = 600 (exact answer: 599)
9 400 × 50 = 20 000 (exact answer: 20016)
10 300 ÷ 50 = 6 (exact answer: 6)
11 300 + 800 = 1100 (exact answer: 1106)
12 600 − 100 = 500 (exact answer: 495)

Unit 16 (pages 36 and 37)

1 3	2 95	3 392

4 90 players
5 84 × 7 or 98 × 6
6 112 500
7 Kim = 500, Megan = 750, Alfie = 250

Unit 17 (pages 38 and 39)

1 1851	5 517	9 7134
2 1625	6 279	10 48 r14
3 1272	7 2822	11 31 r6
4 262	8 5175	12 25

How have I done? (pages 40 and 41)

1 £60
2 Examples: $\frac{2}{8}$, $\frac{2}{6}$, $\frac{2}{5}$
3 28%
4 18
5 a) £151 b) £37.75
6 1, 2, 3, 6, 9, 18
7 4725
8 53
9 a) 56 b) 800 c) 1000
10 a) 0.25 b) 0.75
11 £192
12 48
13 65.26
14 7.01, 0.71, 0.17, 0.1, 0.07
15 a) 7 b) 11.1
16 a) 0.4 b) 1.2
17 90 × 10 = 900
18 846 ÷ 6 = 141 (not 139)
19 £1 doubled 20 times = £1 048 576
20 a) 1071 b) 366 c) 3526 d) 36